IF YOU WERE AT . . .
THE FIRST THANKSGIVING

BY ANNE KAMMA
ILLUSTRATED BY BERT DODSON

SCHOLASTIC INC.

New York   Toronto   London   Auckland   Sydney

Mexico City   New Delhi   Hong Kong   Buenos Aires

ISBN-13: 978-0-439-10566-8
ISBN-10: 0-439-10566-8

Book design by Ursula Albano

19 18 17 16 15 14 13 12   8 9 10 11 12/0

Printed in the U.S.A.
First Scholastic printing, October 2001

For Ellen

ACKNOWLEDGMENTS

With grateful thanks to Jim Baker, Plimoth Plantation historian, for generously reviewing the manuscript, and to Carolyn Freeman Travers, research manager, Plimoth Plantation, Plymouth, Massachusetts; the Smithsonian National Museum of the American Indian; Becky Koppelman, Bloomingdale Branch, New York Public Library; the Bancroft Public Library in Salem, New York; the Bank Street Bookstore, New York City; and to my wonderful editor, Eva Moore.

Go Back in Time

Would you like to see what a Pilgrim village or a Wampanoag Indian home was like in Pilgrim times? Would you like to explore the *Mayflower II*? You can, if you visit the Plimoth Plantation in Plymouth, Massachusetts.

Write to: Plimoth Plantation   Or visit: www.plimoth.org
             P.O. Box 1620
             Plymouth, MA 02362

CONTENTS

How it all began

In 1620, a small group of people landed on the coast of Massachusetts. They were the Pilgrims, and they had come from England to make a new home in America. At that time, there were no other Europeans living in New England — the Pilgrims were the very first to settle there.

Their ship, the *Mayflower,* arrived late in the year. It was winter, and the settlers had to build their houses in the snow and freezing rain. Even their temporary home on the *Mayflower* was cold and damp.

Everyone was coughing and getting sick. Many came down with pneumonia. By spring, half the Pilgrims had died. Only fifty-two people were left. Twenty-two of them were children under the age of sixteen.

The Pilgrims, however, refused to give up. They wanted to stay in Plymouth. But could they survive in this wild new land? Could they grow enough food? Would the Indians who lived there attack them?

By fall, they had their answer. Their fields were full of ripe corn and other vegetables. Now there was enough food to last through the winter. And there was peace with their Indian neighbors.

To celebrate, the Pilgrims decided to have a big party — a harvest festival. And they invited their new Indian friends to join them. For the Pilgrims knew that without the Indians' help, they would never have survived.

Today we call that harvest festival the First Thanksgiving.

Why did the Pilgrims come to America?

King James of England said that *everybody* had to belong to the Church of England. If you were caught criticizing the Church or starting your own church, you were in big trouble. You could be sent to jail, or even hanged.

People who wanted to change, or "purify," the Church of England were called Puritans. Most of the Puritans didn't want to leave the Church of England, but there was a small group that did. They wanted a separate church all their own. So they were called Separatists.

When the *Mayflower* sailed for America, half of all the Pilgrims onboard were Puritan Separatists. They were going to America to find a safe place to worship.

The rest of the Pilgrims on the *Mayflower* were not Puritans. They belonged to the Church of England. But life in England was very hard. Many people couldn't find jobs or buy land. Maybe in America, they thought, life would be better.

Who had lived in Plymouth before the Pilgrims?

The Patuxet Indians had lived in Plymouth for thousands of years. They belonged to the Wampanoag (*wam-pa*-NO-*ag*) nation — a tribe that lived in parts of Massachusetts and Rhode Island. Of course, it wasn't called Plymouth then. That was what the Englishman John Smith had named it when he visited in 1614. The Indians had always called it Patuxet, which means "at the little falls."

Every spring, the Indians came to Patuxet to farm and fish. Each family had to grow enough food for the cold months ahead. In the fall, after the harvest, everybody moved back inland to their winter homes.

But a few years before the Pilgrims came, disaster struck. A great sickness killed most of the Indians along the New England coast. The sickness was brought by Europeans who had been fishing and traveling up and down the coast for about a hundred years.

The Indians had no natural defenses against this new disease. In some villages, so many died that there was nobody left to bury the dead. Skulls and bones lay scattered on the ground.

This great sickness also killed the Patuxet Indians. By the time the Pilgrims arrived in Plymouth, nobody had lived there for four years.

Did the Pilgrims have to clear the land?

No. When the Pilgrims arrived in Plymouth, they found all the old cornfields that the Patuxet Indians had made. So they didn't have to clear the land of trees and rocks. All they had to do was get rid of the weeds that had grown in the last four years.

What would your house be like?

Crowded! There were only seven small houses to live in. So everyone had to squeeze in together. You might have had four or five extra people living with your family.

Each house had only one room, called the hall. The hall was your kitchen, bedroom, dining room, and your living room. There was also a loft upstairs, but that was used for storage.

The furniture got moved around a lot. When it was time to eat, out came the wooden benches and boards that were used to make a table.

At night, the benches and boards were placed against the walls. Out came the lumpy mattresses, which were laid right on the cold dirt floor.

If you were one of the lucky ones, your family might have a real bed. Your parents slept on top and you slept in the "trundle" bed hidden underneath. It was like a big drawer that was pulled out at bedtime.

Your house was dark inside. You couldn't see anything out of the tiny windows because they were made from oiled cloth, not glass.

And it was smelly! The air was full of smoke from the fish-oil lamps and from the big fireplace, where something was cooking all day long.

Would you go to school?

There weren't any schools in Plymouth. But that didn't worry the Pilgrims. They thought you could be taught what you needed right in your own home. If you could write your name, do a little math, and read one page from the Bible, you were done with schooling.

Of course, your religious instructions continued. In the evening, it was your father's job to explain the Sunday sermon and the Bible to you. When you got older, you would probably be able to read the whole Bible by yourself.

There were no spelling rules or dictionaries in those days. You spelled a word the way it sounded to you. People might spell *your* name in many different ways.

Every family had to work very hard — even the children. So, there wasn't much time for schooling that first year in Plymouth.

Were Pilgrim parents strict?

Pilgrim parents loved their children, but they were very strict with them. Parents believed it was their job to be sure their children grew up to be good Christians. That meant children could not be allowed to become stubborn or independent.

Children were taught to obey their parents and never say "no" or get angry at them. The Pilgrims believed in following the word of the Bible, which says to "honor your father and your mother." Boys and girls had to bow and curtsy to their parents to show respect.

When you grew up, you *still* had to obey your parents. It was the law. If you broke the law, you could be punished.

What happened when the Pilgrims and the Indians met?

The Pilgrims had wanted to meet and trade with their Indian neighbors, but the Indians had stayed away. Then one warm spring day, a tall Indian wearing only a leather breechcloth walked right into Plymouth. The Pilgrims were even more amazed when he said, "Welcome, Englishmen!"

He spoke English! But was he a spy? Were the Indians about to attack? No. The man was very friendly. His name was Samoset, and he had learned English from traveling fishermen whom he had met along the New England coast.

Samoset told the Pilgrims all about their neighbors, the Wampanoag tribe, and about their most important chief, Massasoit (*mas-uh*-SOH-*it*). He also told them about the great sickness. Now the Pilgrims knew how the land had been cleared. And they knew that the Patuxet Indians would never return.

Did Chief Massasoit want peace?

Samoset came back to Plymouth a week later. This time he brought Chief Massasoit and sixty men armed with bows and arrows. Captain Myles Standish and his small band of men stood ready with their muskets.

But Massasoit had come in peace.

The Pilgrims thought of Massasoit as a king, and they gave him a knife and a copper chain with a jewel in it. They told him that King James wanted to be his friend and ally. They said that they wanted to trade with the Wampanoag people.

This pleased Massasoit. So the Pilgrims' governor, John Carver, sat down with Massasoit and made a peace treaty. They agreed not to attack one another. Anything that was stolen would be returned. Hurting someone from the other group was not allowed — the one who caused the injury would be punished. And if outsiders attacked one group, the other would help them fight off the enemy.

When they were done, Massasoit's men applauded and the Pilgrims were happy. This was a treaty that helped both the Indians and the Pilgrims.

Were you safe after the peace treaty?

Yes. Now you could work in the cornfields or go berry picking with the other children and not worry about being attacked. The treaty made all the Pilgrims feel safe.

The Wampanoag felt safe, too. The great sickness had killed many of their warriors. Now the Pilgrims, with their powerful guns, would help them if they were ever attacked by their enemies, the Narragansett.

The Wampanoag brought their wives and children to visit Plymouth. One Pilgrim made special mention of this in a letter. "We often go to them, and they come to us," he wrote.

You might even have played with some of the visiting Wampanaog children.

The peace with the Wampanoag lasted more than fifty years — so long that your children and your grandchildren might have been born during the time of peace.

Who was Squanto?

Samoset brought another visitor — a man who spoke even better English than he did. This man's name was Tisquantum, or Squanto, and he was a Patuxet Indian.

Squanto had been captured by an English sea captain and sold into slavery in Spain. After he escaped, he came back to America on an English ship. But by the time he returned home, his people had died of the great sickness.

Squanto decided to stay in Plymouth and help the Pilgrims. He became their guide and translator, and he showed them how to catch fish and find food. The Pilgrims called their new friend "a special instrument sent of God."

Was there a special way to grow corn?

The Pilgrims had never grown corn before, but they learned how to do it the Indian way. You had to plant a few corn seeds under a little hill of soil. Squanto showed them a trick for making the corn grow better: You put some fish under the seeds before covering them with dirt. The Indians knew that rotting fish make great fertilizer.

Catching the fish, called alewives, was easy. Each spring the alewives swam up Town Brook, which ran right through Plymouth. There were so many that even the children could scoop them up by the bucketful.

The Pilgrims planted twenty acres of corn, so they had to scoop up about 20,000 fish!

What else did the Pilgrims grow?

The men planted fields of wheat, peas, barley, and Indian corn. The women and children planted herbs and vegetables in their small gardens.

The Pilgrims had brought seeds with them on the *Mayflower.* But some of the English seeds didn't grow very well in Plymouth. All the pea plants died in the hot sun. The wheat did poorly, and the barley only a little better. Only the garden vegetables, like carrots, turnips, and onions, came out well.

It was the plants they got from the Indians — the corn, beans, squash, and pumpkins — that gave the Pilgrims most of their food. They planted them right next to one another in the fields, the Indian way.

Did the children have to work?

Yes, children worked, too. There were lots of things for them to do.

They picked wild berries and beach plums.

They fed the chickens and hunted for fresh eggs.

They weeded the vegetable gardens.

They threw rocks at the foxes in the cornfields to keep them from digging up the fish, and chased off the blackbirds.

They caught eels in the streams by pushing them out of the mud with their bare feet and then grabbing them with their hands — just as Squanto taught them.

By age six, boys started working more in the fields with their fathers, and girls in the house with their mothers.

Was the first harvest a success?

The fall harvest was a *big* success. Now the Pilgrims had enough food to last them through the winter. Each person would get more than four cups of cornmeal a day.

All the corn was stored in the Common House next to the fish, meat, and vegetables.

There were no refrigerators or freezers in those days. But the Pilgrims knew how to keep food from spoiling.

They packed the fish and meat in salt, or smoked it over the fire. Children cut pumpkins and other vegetables into strips and hung them up to dry. Eels, eggs, and cucumbers (called "cow cumbers") were pickled in vinegar and put in barrels. Pickled cow cumbers were a favorite treat for the children.

Why did the Pilgrims want to celebrate?

They had all worked very, very hard. Now the harvest was finished, and food was safely stored away for the winter. The Pilgrims wanted to celebrate with a harvest festival, just like those they used to have in England. It was time to stop working for a few days, and just eat and have fun!

Nobody went to church on the First Thanksgiving, because a harvest festival wasn't a religious holiday. In fact, the Pilgrims never called it "Thanksgiving" at all. They just called it a harvest festival. If you had said "Happy Thanksgiving" to the Pilgrims, they wouldn't have known what you were talking about.

Who made Thanksgiving a national holiday?

As America grew, it became a tradition to celebrate harvest time as a kind of thanksgiving. But people didn't always celebrate on the same day. For example, in 1705 one town in Connecticut waited to have its harvest festival until the molasses needed for making pies arrived from the West Indies.

In 1863, President Abraham Lincoln signed a proclamation declaring Thanksgiving a national holiday. He even picked the day for celebrating it: Thursday.

Today, all Americans celebrate Thanksgiving on the same day — the last Thursday in November.

Were there also special days for thanking God?

Yes. If the Pilgrims felt that God had been especially good to them, they declared a religious holiday. They called it a "Day of Thanksgiving and Praise."

Then everyone in the village stopped working and spent the day in church praising God. On a Day of Thanksgiving and Praise you couldn't sing and dance or play with your friends, like you could at a harvest festival. This was a time to be serious and humble before God.

What was the first thing the Pilgrims did to get ready for their harvest festival?

The Pilgrims knew they would need lots of food. So the new governor, William Bradford, sent out four men to shoot ducks and geese and other wildfowl.

Because it was fall, there were hundreds of migrating birds wintering over in Plymouth Bay. It took the men just one day to bring back enough food to feed the whole village for almost a week.

Who were the surprise guests?

Chief Massasoit came. And he brought along ninety of his men! The Pilgrims were worried. How were they going to feed all their new guests?

But Chief Massosoit solved the problem. He sent some of his men out hunting. They brought back five deer. Now there was plenty of food for everyone.

Who was in charge of cooking?

Four women supervised all the cooking for about 150 people.

There were very few women in Plymouth at this time. Eighteen had come over on the *Mayflower,* but most had died in the terrible first winter.

The four cooks had help from the few servants who had been brought by Pilgrim families, and the children helped, too.

Was the food cooked outdoors?

No. Although many pictures show the Pilgrims working over big outdoor fires, actually most of the food was cooked in people's houses the English way.

Each house had a huge fireplace with pots and pans hanging down over the open fire. You could cook just about anything there — meats, fish, stews, soups, and desserts.

To roast the meat, you first had to cut it into pieces. The Pilgrims never roasted a deer whole. They speared the pieces of meat on long iron rods, called spits. The spit handles were turned slowly so that the meat cooked on all sides.

Turning the spit was usually a job for a child. It took so many hours for the meat to cook, you'd get really hot and tired. And it was dark and smoky inside the house.

If you were lucky, you might get to help with the bread baking instead. Bread was baked outdoors in a big clay oven. You'd be outside in the fresh air, where you could watch everyone rushing to get ready for the big feast.

How did the children help?

They carried water from the spring . . .
. . . brought vegetables in from the garden . . .
. . . tended the fires . . . stirred the stews . . .
. . . cut up the squash and pumpkins . . .
. . . ground the spices . . . sliced the eels . . .
. . . and much more!

Would you have taken a bath to get ready for the big celebration?

No. The Pilgrims hated baths. They thought that too many baths washed away the body's protection against disease.

Scientists in 1621 didn't know what we know today — that dirt has germs in it that can make you sick.

The Pilgrims took only a few baths a year. So if you were a Pilgrim, you would look and smell a lot dirtier than you do today.

How many Pilgrim children were at the First Thanksgiving?

Probably twenty-two.

Even though many adults had died during the first winter, most of the children had survived. So almost half the Pilgrims at the First Thanksgiving were children age sixteen and younger.

The children had worked very, very hard. Now it was time for them to have fun, too!

Did any Indian children come to the First Thanksgiving?

We don't know for sure if Chief Massasoit brought along any children.

But there was one Indian family living in Plymouth: the Hobbamock family. They lived right across the brook on the south side of the village.

Hobbamock was a warrior and counselor who was sent by Chief Massasoit to live with the Pilgrims. His job was to be an ambassador for his people. Like Squanto, Hobbamock became a good friend to the Pilgrims and lived in Plymouth the rest of his life. Perhaps some of his children played with the Pilgrim children. Perhaps some of them were friends.

We don't know how many children Hobbamock had, or if the whole family came to the First Thanksgiving — but it's quite possible they did.

What did the Pilgrims wear?

If you were a boy under seven years old, you wore a long dress, just like the girls. And you wore a cap, called a big-gin, which tied under your chin.

By the time you turned seven, you wore what adults wore. This picture shows what you and your family might have worn at the First Thanksgiving. As you can see, the Pilgrims liked colorful clothes.

For underwear, you wore a long shirt called a shift. You wore long stockings, but nobody wore underpants.

Girls had long hair, just like their mothers. Most of the time you stuffed your hair inside a little cap, called a coif. You wore your coif indoors and out. If you needed a hat for the sun or the cold, you put it right on top of your coif.

Putting on your shoes was easy, because you didn't have to worry about which shoe went on your left foot and which went on your right. The Pilgrims' shoes were all cut the same.

What did the Wampanoag Indians wear?

Everyone except boys under ten wore a deerskin breech-cloth around the waist. It was a belt with flaps hanging down the front and back. Girls wore deerskin skirts over their breechcloths, just like their mothers did.

Deerskin mantles were often worn by both children and adults. You'd wrap the mantle around you and fasten it over one shoulder. Then you'd tie a belt around your waist to keep it in place.

When you were old enough, you wore your knife in a sheath that hung around your neck.

The picture on page 42 shows what the Wampanoag might have worn at the First Thanksgiving. Although today we celebrate Thanksgiving at the end of November, we don't know exactly when the First Thanksgiving took place. We do know it happened sometime between September 21st and November 9th. If it was a warm day, you wouldn't have worn moccasins. Everyone would have preferred to go barefoot, just like many of the Pilgrims did.

If it was a cold day, you would have worn leggings, and maybe a fur robe.

Where did the Pilgrims and Indians eat?

In the middle of the street, just like the Pilgrims had done back in England for their village celebrations.

Nobody had a house that was big enough to seat 150 people for dinner. So the Pilgrims set up their tables right in the middle of their only street, which they called "The Street."

It was like a giant picnic.

Were there enough tables and chairs?

The Pilgrims had left their tables and chairs behind when they sailed for America. There was no room on the *Mayflower* for all that furniture. They had to make new furniture when they arrived in Plymouth.

Luckily, there were plenty of barrels and boxes and wooden boards. So that's what they used for furniture.

They put boards on top of the barrels: That was the table. Then they covered the tables with beautiful linen tablecloths.

They sat on benches made of boards held up by tree stumps or small boxes and barrels.

Who served the food?

It was the children's job to carry food from the kitchen to the table and to serve their own families. The few servants also helped serve.

You couldn't eat until you finished serving. And you couldn't sit down when you were ready to eat. Children had to eat standing up. Only adults got to sit down while they ate.

What did you do before you started to eat?

You got out your *big* dinner napkin.

The Pilgrims ate mostly with their fingers. Nobody used forks, because there weren't any forks in those days. Forks weren't used until many years later. But eating with your fingers could get very messy. That's why you needed a big napkin.

The napkins were squares of cloth, three feet wide by three feet long. If you held your napkin up around your neck, it might reach almost to your ankles.

There was a rule for using your napkin. You had to wipe your fingers *before* taking food from the pot in the middle of the table. Otherwise the food in the pot got dirty from everyone's fingers.

You also used your napkin to hold pieces of hot meat so you wouldn't burn yourself.

You cut your food with your everyday knife. Even children used knives. And you used a spoon when you ate soup or stew. If you didn't own a spoon, you might have eaten your soup with a clam shell attached to a stick.

Would you get enough to eat?

When the Pilgrims first arrived, all they had to eat were hard biscuits, salted meat and fish, moldy cheese, dried peas, and sour beer. The food tasted terrible.

But now the harvest was in, and there was plenty of good food. At the harvest festival you got to eat as much as you wanted!

And that's what the Pilgrims did for almost one week.

Would you eat turkey?

Yes! There was plenty of roasted wild turkey at the First Thanksgiving. And probably stuffing, too, though it didn't taste like the stuffing we eat today. The Pilgrims made their stuffing with cornmeal, and they might have added cranberries. They called it "pudding in the belly."

Had the Pilgrims ever seen turkeys before they came to America?

There were no wild turkeys back in England, but there were tame turkeys that people raised for food. The first tame turkeys came from Mexico. Can you guess how they got to England?

The Mexican Indians knew how to tame wild turkeys. When the Spanish explorers arrived in America in the 1500s, they discovered that they really liked turkey meat. So, they took some Mexican turkeys back to Spain with them.

Pretty soon, all of Europe was raising turkeys. By the time the Pilgrims sailed for America, people in England had been raising turkeys for almost a hundred years. So the Pilgrims knew all about turkeys!

What other foods did they have at the First Thanksgiving?

They ate stewed eels. They ate cod and sea bass, their favorite fish. They ate roasted ducks and geese. They probably even ate roasted swans. And they ate plenty of cornbread. They didn't eat the few pigs they had brought along on the *Mayflower*. They were saving them until they had a bigger herd.

Meat and bread were the Pilgrims' favorite foods. They didn't like vegetables, but they ate them, anyway. Having lived on stale and salty food the first winter, they were grateful for all the new fresh vegetables they had now, such as boiled pumpkins and beans.

Probably the biggest treat at the festival was the deer meat the Indians had supplied.

Why was deer meat so special?

In England, only rich people ate deer meat. They killed the deer in their own private forests, where no one else was allowed to hunt.

The Pilgrims were not rich. They were just ordinary people. So they had never tasted deer meat before they came to America. But here they could eat as much of it as they could get. Here nobody owned the deer in the forest.

What foods did the Pilgrims hate to eat?

Clams and mussels. There were lots of them, but the Pilgrims ate them only when there was nothing else. These shellfish were considered poor people's food, and "the meanest of God's blessings," according to one visitor to Plymouth. The Pilgrims fed clams and mussels to their pigs.

With so many other tasty foods to eat at the Thanksgiving feast, do you think the Pilgrims would have wanted to eat clams and mussels, too?

Did the Pilgrims make cranberry sauce?

There were cranberries all around Plymouth, and they were easy to pick. So why didn't the Pilgrims make cranberry sauce?

They had no sugar. Try eating a raw cranberry — it's very sour. Unless cooked with something sweet, it tastes terrible.

The Pilgrims didn't get sugar until long after the First Thanksgiving. Even then they had very little of it, and it was used mostly as a seasoning (like salt) rather than for cooking and baking.

Did they drink beer at the First Thanksgiving?

In those days, people usually drank beer every day. But we don't know for sure if there was any beer at the First Thanksgiving.

The Pilgrims had run out of the beer they had brought on the *Mayflower* long before their harvest feast. Perhaps they had time to make new beer after they had harvested their barley. Beer is made from barley malt.

If they didn't have beer to drink, they probably drank water. There was a spring of pure water in the middle of Plymouth Village. The Pilgrims were surprised to discover how sweet and delicious clean water like that tasted. They drank from the spring every day.

The Pilgrims also loved apple cider. But there weren't any apples in Plymouth yet, so they wouldn't have had cider for the feast. And there wasn't any coffee or tea. The Pilgrims had never tasted coffee or tea. People in England didn't know about these drinks until thirty years later when traders came from Africa and China.

And you would not have drunk milk at the First Thanksgiving, either. The Pilgrims had no cows, and the milk they got from any goats they might have brought with them would have been used to make butter and cheese.

Did the Pilgrims think drinking beer was wrong?

No. The Pilgrims were very religious. They thought it was a sin to get drunk. But they did drink beer. They drank it because it was safer than water.

Most of the water in England was polluted in the early 1600s. You could get very sick from it. But beer was safe because it has alcohol in it, and alcohol kills germs. So, that's what people drank every day.

But their beer was not like beer today. The women made it at home. There was very little alcohol in it, so you wouldn't get drunk from drinking it with your food.

People had beer for breakfast, lunch, and dinner. They thought it was good for you. Children started drinking it as soon as they were able to hold a cup in their hands.

When was it time for dessert?

Anytime! You could eat your dessert before your meat and vegetables if you liked. Your parents wouldn't mind.

The Pilgrims put all the food on the table at once — soups, stews, bread, meat, vegetables, desserts. It didn't matter which you ate first.

But the desserts at the First Thanksgiving weren't like the desserts we eat today. You might not have liked them very much, because they weren't very sweet. The Pilgrims didn't have the sugar or molasses needed to make sweet cakes or pies.

And they didn't have honey, either. There were no honeybees in New England when the Pilgrims first arrived. Honeybees were brought over later by the English settlers. The Indians had never seen such things before. They called the bees "Englishmen's flies."

There might have been some dried fruit for dessert, but no fresh fruit. It was too late in the year to pick wild berries and fruit — and the Pilgrims didn't like fresh fruit, anyway. They preferred fruit cooked in puddings. Perhaps you would have eaten cornmeal pudding sweetened with dried strawberries or grapes.

Why didn't the Pilgrims serve pumpkin pie?

Pumpkin pie is one of our favorite Thanksgiving foods. The Pilgrims had pumpkins, and they knew how to make pies — but there were no pumpkin pies at the First Thanksgiving.

Look at the ingredients used to make a pumpkin pie for today's Thanksgiving table. The Pilgrims had only those printed in tan. You need more than pumpkin to make a pumpkin pie!

PUMPKIN PIE

CRUST

1 1/4 cups flour
Flour is made from ground grain, such as wheat or rye. The Pilgrims grew wheat — but they probably did not have enough to make much flour.

1/4 teaspoon salt
The Pilgrims used salt to preserve meat and poultry; they boiled salt water to get their salt.

1/3 cup shortening
Shortening is a kind of fat that is an important ingredient in making pie crusts. The Pilgrims probably got their cooking fat from ducks and geese. This kind of animal fat tastes much different from the vegetable shortening cooks use today.

3-4 tablespoons water
No problem for the Pilgrims; they had a spring right in the middle of town.

FILLING

2 cups mashed pumpkin
Thanks to the Indians, the Pilgrims had plenty of pumpkins!

1/2 cup sugar
1 tablespoon molasses
Sugar and molasses make a pie taste sweet. The Pilgrims didn't have either of these sweeteners.

1/2 teaspoon salt
1/2 teaspoon ground cinnamon
1/4 teaspoon ground ginger
The Pilgrims had salt and spices, but they would have had to grind the cinnamon and ginger by hand. Today we can buy these already ground.

1 cup milk
There were no cows in Plymouth in 1621 — but there might have been some goats.

1 or 2 eggs
It's possible that the Pilgrims had some hens, so they could have had eggs.

Were there medicines to take if you ate too much?

Yes, but the Pilgrims didn't have drugstores. They grew their medicines in their gardens. Their medicines were plants called herbs, and there was an herb for nearly every ailment. If you got a bruise, you put marjoram on it. Rosemary was good for toothaches.

If you ate too much at the feast and got a stomachache, your mother would have made you a drink with peppermint leaves. That probably would have made you feel better in no time.

Marjoram   *Peppermint*

Who had to clean the dishes?

Nobody! The Pilgrims didn't clean their dishes with soap and water the way we do today. The women and girls just rinsed the pottery bowls, wooden platters, cups, knives, and spoons and put them back on the shelf.

Napkins were washed only once a month. You can imagine how dirty they got! But the Pilgrims weren't bothered by dirt the way we are. They were used to it. And doing the laundry was a *really* big job in those days.

First, the women had to make soap out of animal fat and ashes. That took a long time. Then the children had to carry water from the stream, so it could be boiled in big outdoor pots. After everything was washed, the laundry was hung on bushes to dry.

What did the Pilgrims and Indians do after they ate?

They just had fun.

The Pilgrim men put on a parade, marching to the beat of the drum and the sound of the trumpet.

The Wampanoag danced in a long line, led by their great chief, Massasoit.

The children played games similar to hide-and-seek and blindman's buff. Everybody joined in a tug-of-war.

Captain Myles Standish and his men fired their noisy and smoky muskets into the air.

The Indians sang their ancient songs. The Pilgrims sang English folk songs and psalms.

The Pilgrim women danced English country dances to the tune of the hornpipe — but they had to do it without the men. The Pilgrims didn't think that men and women should dance together.

And if there was a footrace, a Wampanoag probably was the winner. They were known to be great runners.

Where did all the guests sleep?

The Indians celebrated with the Pilgrims for three days.

But the Pilgrims didn't have room in their tiny houses for ninety guests to stay overnight. The Wampanoag guests slept outdoors under the stars, or perhaps under some shelters they made out of branches.

Although the Indians were used to sleeping on the ground when they traveled, at home they slept on comfortable wooden beds covered with soft animal skins.

Massasoit was a very important chief, so maybe he stayed with Hobbamock, his special ambassador who lived in Plymouth — *if* Hobbamock had finished building his house by that time.

What might you have heard before falling asleep?

Singing, and it would have been the Wampanoag.

The Indians loved to sing. They sang at their religious ceremonies, they sang as a way of saying "thank you" — and sometimes they sang themselves to sleep. We know this from Edward Winslow, one of the few Pilgrims who slept overnight in Massasoit's village.

What happened to the Pilgrims after the First Thanksgiving?

Not long after the festival, a ship called the *Fortune* arrived from England. It brought thirty-five new settlers, but no food — "not so much as a biscuitcake," wrote Governor Bradford. So, the Pilgrims had to share their food with all the newcomers.

But the Pilgrims were not discouraged. They thought there was much to be thankful for. Less than a year earlier, they had landed in a wild and unknown land. Half of their people had died from hunger and cold the first winter.

Now everything was changed. They had houses to live in. Nobody was sick. And they had learned how to grow food in their new land.

They had found a safe place to worship God. And they were at peace with their Wampanoag neighbors — a peace that lasted fifty years, during which time the little settlement grew and prospered.